100 AMAZING FACTS ABOUT FINLAND

© 2023, Marc Dresgui

Content

Introduction 8

Fact 1 - The Mysterious Dance of the Northern Lights 9

Fact 2 - Reindeer, the king of the Finnish forest 10

Fact 3 - Where is the sun in winter 11

Fact 4 - Endless days in summer 12

Fact 5 - The forest that covers 75% of the country 13

Fact 6 - The Enigma of the 188,000 Lakes 14

Fact 7 - The National Epic: The Kalevala 15

Fact 8 - Finland, a former Swedish territory 16

Fact 9 - Russia's influence on Finland 17

Fact 10 - The sauna, much more than a hot bath 18

Fact 11 - Christmas Eve and its traditions 19

Fact 12 - The mighty Ukko, god of thunder 20

Fact 13 - Mämmi, a delicacy for Easter 21

Fact 14 - Pesäpallo, baseball's Finnish cousin 22

Fact 15 - Paavo Nurmi, the phenomenon of the Olympic Games 23

Fact 16 - Vappu's Brilliant Spring Party 24

Fact 17 - Do Finns really speak Swedish? 25

Fact 18 - One of the best education in the world 26

Fact 19 - How Finland Became Independent 27

Fact 20 - Why Holly Is So Special 28

Fact 21 - The Amazing Wife Babywearing Race 29

Fact 22 - The Mysterious Myth of Sampo 30

Fact 23 - The bear, a sacred animal of folklore 31

Fact 24 - The Magic of the Polar Night..................32

Fact 25 - Kuksa, the traditional wooden cup 33

Fact 26 - The Legend of the Great Hero Väinämöinen..................34

Fact 27 - Thousands of Islands on the Coast 35

Fact 28 - The Challenge of Swimming in the Ice..................36

Fact 29 - Why Finns Love Simplicity..................37

Fact 30 - The secret to well-being in Finland 38

Fact 31 - Salmiakki, a salty treat..................39

Fact 32 - Finland, Ice Hockey Champions 40

Fact 33 - Lapland's Giant Mosquitoes 41

Fact 34 - The Influence of Christianity on Culture 42

Fact 35 - The haunting melodies of the kantele..................43

Fact 36 - The Mysterious Creature of Lake Näsi 44

Fact 37 - The Brave Lemminkäinen and His Adventures..................45

Fact 38 - The Magic of Midsummer Fires..................46

Fact 39 - Finns Ski World Champions 47

Fact 40 - The secret of Finnish longevity..................48

Fact 41 - The Art of Silent Conversation..................49

Fact 42 - Why Are Shoes Left At The Door 50

Fact 43 - Trolls Who Live Under the Mountains 51

Fact 44 - The Power of the Wolf in Legends..................52

Fact 45 - The Log Cabin Tradition..................53

Fact 46 - How the Reindeer Helps Santa Claus 54

Fact 47 - The Beauty of Runic Songs 55

Fact 48 - The Role of Women in Mythology 56

Fact 49 - The Strange Creature of Lake Inari 57

Fact 50 - Pyys, Sacred Birds of the North 58

Fact 51 - Finland's invention of the smart card 59

Fact 52 - The Strange Mud Bath Ritual 60

Fact 53 - Cats of the Finnish Forest 61

Fact 54 - Fairies Dancing in the Meadows 62

Fact 55 - The shortest day of the year 63

Fact 56 - The Mysteries of the Finnish Language 64

Fact 57 - The Legend of the Winter Rainbow 65

Fact 58 - The Ice Fishing Competition 66

Fact 59 - How to Build a Finnish Igloo 67

Fact 60 - The Great Fire of the Autumnal Equinox 68

Fact 61 - The Independence Day Feast 69

Fact 62 - The Treasure Hunt of Legends 70

Fact 63 - Finnish Children's Winter Games 71

Fact 64 - The Miracle of the Singing Ice 72

Fact 65 - The Enchanted Forests of the North 73

Fact 66 - The Role of Stars in Folklore 74

Fact 67 - The Enigma of the Midnight Sun 75

Fact 68 - The Story of the First Finnish School 76

Fact 69 - Why Fish Is So Precious 77

Fact 70 - The Day Finland Stopped Time 78

Fact 71 - The Magical Power of Stones 79

Fact 72 - The Dance of the Will-o'-the-Wisps 80

Fact 73 - The Mystery of the Northern Swamps 81

Fact 74 - The Journey of Migratory Birds 82

Fact 75 - The Soothing Sounds of Nature 83

Fact 76 - The Legend of the Mother of the Forest 84

Fact 77 - The Healing Power of Plants 85

Fact 78 - The Tradition of Cradle Songs 86

Fact 79 - The Magic of Winter's Tales 87

Fact 80 - The Secrets of Lake Saimaa 88

Fact 81 - The Ice Circle Phenomenon 89

Fact 82 - The Reindeer's Journey to the South 90

Fact 83 - The Singing of the Trees in the Wind 91

Fact 84 - The Magic of Shimmering Snow 92

Fact 85 - The History of the First Library 93

Fact 86 - The Legend of the Lake Dragon 94

Fact 87 - The Role of Elders in Culture 95

Fact 88 - The Mystery of the Song of the Earth 96

Fact 89 - The Strange Tradition of Snow Bathing 97

Fact 90 - The Secret of Finnish Strength 98

Fact 91 - Shadows Dancing Under the Moon 99

Fact 92 - The Guardian Spirits of the House 100

Fact 93 - The Dance of the Fireflies in Summer 101

Fact 94 - The Ancient Art of Finnish Weaving 102

Fact 95 - The Beauty of Nature's Ballet 103

Fact 96 - The Legend of the Guardians of the Forest 104

Fact 97 - The Riddle of the Upside Down River 105

Fact 98 - Rituals of Transition from Childhood to Adulthood 106

Fact 99 - The Magic of the First Snows 107

Fact 100 - The Story of Finland's First Winter 108

Conclusion 109

Quiz 110

Answers 116

"Finnish light is second to none. In summer, the sun is a wood fire that never goes out."

— Conan O'Brien

Introduction

Welcome, dear reader, to an odyssey through Finland like you've never seen before. Have you ever felt the curiosity to discover what lies behind the thick forests, shimmering lakes and northern lights of the Far North? Maybe you've heard of Finland for its saunas, reindeer, or passion for design, but this country is full of mysteries, traditions, and stories waiting to be discovered.

Throughout these pages, you will be guided through a series of facts, some surprising, some poetic, but all deeply rooted in the heart and soul of Finland. Each fact will reveal a new aspect of this land to you, bringing you a little closer to its essence and its people.

Whether you're an adventure-hungry traveler, a history buff, or just curious about nature, this book was designed for you. Let yourself be carried away by these stories, and perhaps, by the end of your reading, you will feel a little Finnish yourself.

So, are you ready to dive into the depths of Finland and unveil its most precious secrets? Open your eyes, your heart and your mind wide, and embark with me on this fascinating adventure.

Marc Dresgui

Fact 1 - The Mysterious Dance of the Northern Lights

Have you ever heard of the Northern Lights? It's these beautiful lights that dance in the night sky, especially near the Earth's poles. In Finland, they are a common sight, especially in the north, in Lapland. There, the sky lights up with green, pink, purple or even red, creating a real natural spectacle.

But where do these lights come from? It's a fascinating phenomenon caused by charged particles from the Sun colliding with Earth's atmosphere. When these particles meet oxygen and nitrogen, they create these beautiful colors in the sky. Each color corresponds to a different type of gas: green comes from oxygen at low altitudes, while red is caused by oxygen at high altitudes.

The best time to see them in Finland is during the cold, clear nights between September and March. So, if one day you travel there during this time, don't forget to roll your eyes. You might witness this luminous dance that has fascinated humans for centuries.

Fact 2 - Reindeer, the king of the Finnish forest

Have you ever seen a reindeer in real life? In Finland, these majestic animals are considered the kings of the forest. With their impressive large woods and elegant gait, they roam the vast forests and snow-covered plains of the country. If you're traveling to northern Finland, chances are you'll cross paths with them.

Reindeer are not only beautiful to look at, they also have cultural and economic significance in Finland. The Sami, the indigenous people of northern Scandinavia, have herded reindeer for thousands of years. For them, these animals provide food, fur, and other essential resources.

But did you know that every reindeer in Finland has an owner? Yes, even if they roam freely, they belong to someone. Specific markings on their ears help identify them.

Next time you think of Finland, imagine these magnificent creatures moving freely through forests and snow-capped mountains. They are truly the kings of this magical land.

Fact 3 - Where is the sun in winter

Do you ever wonder where the sun goes in winter? In Finland, during one time of the year, the sun doesn't rise at all in the north! This is known as the "polar night". Imagine living in a place where, for several weeks, the sun never rises. It's a truly unique experience.

This happens because Finland is located so close to the North Pole. During the winter, the country is tilted in such a way that part of its territory, especially in the north, is shaded by the sun. Conversely, in summer, there is the "midnight sun" where the sun never sets for days or even weeks in some parts of the country.

But how do Finns adapt to this strange phenomenon? Many use special lights in their homes to mimic daylight. And the snow, which usually covers the ground in winter, reflects the slightest light, illuminating the landscapes.

So, even though the sun plays hide and seek in the winter, Finland still finds ways to shine in some way.

Fact 4 - Endless days in summer

Imagine having a day that never ends. How would you feel if the sun refused to set for days or even weeks? In summer, this is exactly what happens in northern Finland. This fascinating phenomenon is called the "midnight sun".

Thanks to Finland's position near the Arctic Circle, the sun remains visible 24 hours a day for a period in summer. Imagine having a picnic, playing or even reading a book at midnight with the sun still high in the sky! It's an experience that many Finns cherish and look forward to every year.

But that's not all. This midnight sun gives nature an incredible energy. Plants grow faster, and animals are more active. The lakes and rivers, sparkling in the constant sun, offer a spectacle of breathtaking beauty.

So, if you ever find yourself in Finland during the summer, don't forget to enjoy these endless days. It's a magic that only a few places in the world can offer.

Fact 5 - The forest that covers 75% of the country

Have you ever dreamed of getting lost in a huge forest? In Finland, this dream can easily become a reality. Unbelievable but true: forests cover about 75% of the country! It is one of the most forested areas in Europe. Imagine, almost three-quarters of Finland is green and full of trees.

These vast expanses of forest play a vital role for Finns. Not only do they provide a home for a wide variety of wildlife, but they also serve as a resource for the timber industry, which is one of the largest in the country. Without these forests, Finland would not be the same.

When you walk through these woods, you can feel the calm and peace they exude. Many Finns find it a source of relaxation and well-being. They pick berries, fish, or just go for a walk, enjoying the beauty of nature.

If you're wondering what Europe's green lung is, think of Finland. With its dense and green forests, it exudes life and freshness like nowhere else.

Fact 6 - The Enigma of the 188,000 Lakes

Have you ever wondered how many lakes a country can have? Finland may hold the answer with its impressive 188,000 lakes! Yes, you heard that right. From small hidden ponds to vast expanses of water, this country is truly the kingdom of lakes.

These lakes were formed thousands of years ago, at the end of the last ice age, when huge glaciers melted and hollowed out the earth's surface. Today, they are an essential part of the Finnish landscape. The largest of these, Lake Saimaa, is so vast that it almost resembles a sea.

Not only do these lakes offer scenic beauty, but they are also the heart of many activities. In summer, Finns enjoy swimming, fishing or boating. In winter, when they freeze over, these lakes turn into natural skating rinks where you can skate or fish through the ice.

So, the next time you think of a land of water, remember Finland. With its countless shimmering lakes, it is a place where water meets land in the most spectacular way.

Fact 7 - The National Epic: The Kalevala

Do you know the legends that shape a country? Finland has a national epic that has captivated the hearts of its people for generations: the "Kalevala". It is a collection of ancient poems that recounts the exploits of mythical heroes, love adventures and magical quests.

The "Kalevala" was compiled in the 19th century by Elias Lönnrot, a physician and researcher, who traveled across the country to collect these traditional songs. Thanks to him, these oral histories, passed down from generation to generation, have been preserved and shared with the world.

One of the most famous heroes of the "Kalevala" is Väinämöinen, a sage with magical powers who plays the kantele, a traditional Finnish instrument. His adventures and those of the other characters have inspired many artists, musicians and writers, not only in Finland, but also around the world.

If you like epic tales of magic, love and adventure, immerse yourself in the "Kalevala". It is a window into the soul and culture of Finland, a treasure that continues to enchant to this day.

Fact 8 - Finland, a former Swedish territory

Did you know that, for centuries, Finland was not its own country, but part of Sweden? Yes, that's right! Before becoming independent, Finland was under Swedish rule for almost 600 years, from the Middle Ages until the early 19th century.

During this period, Finnish culture, politics and society were greatly influenced by Sweden. Many Finnish cities were founded by the Swedes, and the castles and fortresses built at that time still show the imprint of Swedish architecture today.

Swedish, by the way, is still one of Finland's two official languages, along with Finnish. In some coastal regions, such as the Åland archipelago, Swedish is even the main language. It is a living testament to these centuries of close ties between the two nations.

So, the next time you hear about Finland, remember its Swedish past. It is an essential part of Finnish history, which has shaped the country as we know it today.

Fact 9 - Russia's influence on Finland

After being under Swedish influence, did you know that Finland was also strongly influenced by Russia? In 1809, after the war between Sweden and Russia, Finland became an autonomous Grand Duchy under the Russian Empire. This new status lasted for just over a century, until Finnish independence in 1917.

During this period, Finland retained a great deal of autonomy, with its own legal system, currency, and parliament. But Russian influence was felt in many areas. For example, the magnificent Helsinki Cathedral, with its golden domes, is a shining example of Russian architecture of the time.

Although Finland eventually chose the path of independence, relations with Russia have always been important. The border between the two countries is one of the longest in Europe, and cultural, economic and political exchanges have always been frequent.

Thus, just like Sweden, Russia has left an indelible mark on Finland. The history of these two powerful neighbours has shaped Finland's destiny, forging its unique identity.

Fact 10 - The sauna, much more than a hot bath

Have you ever heard of the sauna? In Finland, it's not just a place to relax after a long day. It's a deep-rooted tradition, an almost sacred ritual that dates back thousands of years.

The word "sauna" itself is Finnish, and in this country there are more saunas than cars! That's how important they are. In the past, saunas were even where babies were born and where traditional healers practiced their skills.

But it's not just a hot room. It is an experience that purifies the body and mind. After sweating, it's common to go outside and take a dip in a cool lake or river, even in winter! Some Finns also like to gently flog themselves with birch branches to stimulate circulation.

The sauna is therefore much more than a hot bath. For Finns, it's a way to connect with nature, recharge their batteries and get together with friends and family. A tradition that warms the heart as much as the body!

Fact 11 - Christmas Eve and its traditions

Imagine a Christmas party covered in a thick layer of snow, with melodious carols and soft lights everywhere. In Finland, Christmas Eve is the most anticipated time of the year. It is a time of magic, ancient stories and warm traditions.

One of these traditions is visiting cemeteries to honor the deceased. Finns light candles on the graves of their loved ones, creating a truly breathtaking light show in the polar night. This solemn moment is a way of remembering and getting closer to the ancestors.

Food also plays a central role. Traditional dishes such as "joulukinkku", a Christmas ham, or "riisipuuro", a rice porridge, are served on New Year's Eve. And let's not forget the "glögi", a spicy hot drink, which warms the heart and soul.

And of course, Finland is Santa's home country! The children eagerly await his visit, listening to the crackling of the fire and hoping to hear the tinkling of the sleigh bells.

Fact 12 - The mighty Ukko, god of thunder

Have you ever felt the chill of a thunderstorm, heard the rumble of thunder, and seen lightning streak across the sky? In Finland, this force of nature is associated with Ukko, the supreme god of the Finnish pantheon, ruler of the sky, thunderstorms and thunder.

In ancient Finnish mythology, Ukko was respected and feared. When people needed rain for their crops, they would invoke Ukko, hoping that her power would bring the nourishing clouds. On the other hand, during violent storms, they prayed for his mercy.

It is interesting to note that Ukko had a special instrument, the "Ukonvasara", or Ukko's hammer. Similar to Thor's hammer in Norse mythology, it was used to create lightning bolts. Every time he struck with it, a bolt of lightning flashed, lighting up the sky.

Even though most Finns no longer believe in these old myths, Ukko's imprint remains. With every storm, one can imagine the mighty god of thunder, high in the heavens, wielding his awesome hammer and ruling over the elements.

Fact 13 - Mämmi, a delicacy for Easter

If you're looking for a unique treat to celebrate Easter in Finland, look no further than "mämmi". At first glance, this sweetness may seem a little strange to you, as it looks like mud. But don't be fooled by its appearance!

Mämmi is a sweet preparation made from rye, water, molasses and salt. It is traditionally served cold and is often accompanied by cream or sugar. Although its texture is somewhat gelatinous, its taste is mild and malty, making it a real treat for many.

This delicacy is very old. Finns have been preparing and eating mämmi for centuries during Easter festivities. Originally, as it was a fasting food, it was prepared on Good Friday and kept until Easter.

Today, even if you're not in Finland during Easter, you might be lucky enough to find mämmi in some specialty grocery stores. If you find any, dare to try it! Who knows, you might be pleasantly surprised by this ancient Finnish delicacy.

Fact 14 - Pesäpallo, baseball's Finnish cousin

Have you ever heard of the pesäpallo? If baseball sounds familiar, its Finnish cousin, pesäpallo, might surprise you with its unique rules and distinct style of play.

Conceived in 1922 by Lauri "Tahko" Pihkala, the sport combines elements of traditional baseball with Finnish specificities. One of the main differences is the way the ball is thrown. Instead of throwing the ball horizontally like in baseball, pesäpallo, the pitcher throws the ball directly into the air!

The pesäpallo courts also have a unique shape, resembling a trapezoid. This particular shape influences the strategy of the game, as players can run in different directions after hitting the ball. This makes the game fast-paced, unpredictable, and very exciting to watch.

If you travel to Finland during the summer, you might be lucky enough to see a pesäpallo match. It's a sporting experience that you won't soon forget and that will show you another side of Finnish sports traditions!

Fact 15 - Paavo Nurmi, the phenomenon of the Olympic Games

Do you know Paavo Nurmi? If you're a fan of athletics, his name should ring a bell. Originally from Finland, he is one of the most famous runners in the history of the Olympic Games.

Paavo Nurmi, nicknamed "the Flying Finn", dominated long-distance and middle-distance races in the 1920s. His running technique and stamina were unmatched in his time, and he won a total of nine gold medals and three silver medals at the Olympic Games.

He wasn't just a champion on the track. Nurmi was also known for his methodical approach to training, even using a stopwatch to make sure he maintained the right pace during his races. Through this discipline, he set 22 official world records in athletics.

If you're looking for inspiration in sports, turn to Paavo Nurmi. His dedication, talent and love for running made him a legend, and he remains one of the most iconic figures in Finnish athletics.

Fact 16 - Vappu's Brilliant Spring Party

Did you know that Finns have a very special way of celebrating the arrival of spring? This festival, called Vappu, is one of the largest and most colorful celebrations in Finland.

Every year on May 1st, the streets are filled with people, laughter and music. People wear white hats, symbols of the end of high school, and the atmosphere is filled with joy and anticipation for the warm months ahead.

But it's not just a party! It is also an opportunity to enjoy traditional food and drinks. Finns love to enjoy "tippaleipä", a kind of doughnut shaped like filaments, and "sima", a homemade sparkling soft drink.

So, if you happen to be in Finland at the beginning of May, don't forget to join the Vappu party. Let yourself be carried away by the music, dancing and merriment that celebrate the arrival of spring the Finnish way!

Fact 17 - Do Finns really speak Swedish?

Have you ever heard that some Finns speak Swedish? It's true! Although Finnish is the main language, Swedish also plays an important role in Finland.

In fact, Swedish is one of Finland's two official languages, along with Finnish. This means that many things, such as road signs and official documents, are written in both languages. Impressive, isn't it?

However, not everyone in Finland is fluent in Swedish. Only about 5% of the population is Swedish-speaking. They live mainly on the west coast and in the southwestern archipelago of Finland.

So the next time you hear someone speaking Swedish in Finland, you'll know why. It is living proof of Finland's rich and interconnected history with its Nordic neighbours. And if you decide to learn a few words in Swedish, you might just surprise some Finns!

Fact 18 - One of the best education in the world

Have you ever heard of the Finnish education system? It is recognized as one of the best in the world. And it's not just a slogan, it's proven by many international studies.

What makes Finnish education so special is its student-centered approach. Here, it's not about memorizing to pass an exam, but about understanding and learning to think for yourself. For example, children start school at the age of seven and they have no formal homework for the first few years.

Finland also relies on the quality of its teachers. Did you know that becoming a teacher is one of the most sought-after careers in Finland? They are selected from among the best and receive high-level training.

So, the next time you're wondering why Finland is often cited as a model for education, think about this unique combination: a student-centred approach and exceptionally well-trained teachers. It's truly a winning formula!

Fact 19 - How Finland Became Independent

Do you know how Finland gained its independence? For centuries, this northern territory was under foreign domination, mainly from Sweden and Russia.

At the beginning of the 20th century, when Finland was under the Russian Empire, tensions were rising. The Russian Revolution of 1917 created political chaos, providing an opportunity for Finland. It was in this context that, on 6 December 1917, the Finnish Parliament adopted the Declaration of Independence.

But the road to independence was not easy. After this declaration, the country was shaken by a civil war in 1918 between the "Reds", mainly socialists, and the "Whites", conservatives. The "Whites" eventually won, consolidating Finnish independence.

Today, December 6 is celebrated in Finland as Independence Day. Walking through the streets of Finland on this day, you'd see candles lit in the windows, a poignant symbol of how far the country has come to freedom.

Fact 20 - Why Holly Is So Special

Have you ever wondered why holly holds such a special place in Finnish culture? Its presence in Finland is no coincidence.

Holly is considered a magical plant in many cultures, but in Finland its importance is reinforced by ancient legends. According to one of them, holly protected homes from evil spirits during the dark time of the year, especially during the winter solstice.

But that's not all. In addition to its spiritual symbolism, holly is also known for its medicinal properties. Finns have long used its berries and leaves in traditional medicines. For example, an infusion of holly berries is sometimes consumed to relieve headaches.

The next time you're walking around Finland and come across a holly, take a moment to admire it. This plant, with its prickly leaves and red berries, is not only beautiful but also steeped in a rich cultural and traditional history.

Fact 21 - The Amazing Wife Babywearing Race

Have you ever heard of a competition where men carry their wives or partners on their backs to run? In Finland, it's an authentic tradition and a long-awaited sporting event!

The origin of this race dates back more than two hundred years. Some say it was born out of raids by raiders who robbed women from nearby villages. Today, it's a good-natured race, where couples compete on an obstacle course, with the woman being carried astride her partner's shoulder or spilled onto her partner's back.

The Wife Portage Race, which takes place in Sonkajärvi, is not just a local event: it attracts participants from all over the world. And the price? The winner walks away with the equivalent of his wife's weight in beer, which leads some couples to devise fun strategies to maximize their chances.

So, if you're looking for a truly unique Finnish experience, why not consider participating in or attending this race on your next trip to Finland? It's a guarantee of laughter and memorable memories.

Fact 22 - The Mysterious Myth of Sampo

Do you ever delve into the myths and legends of ancient cultures? If so, you'll be intrigued by the Sampo, a mysterious relic at the heart of Finnish mythology.

Sampo is often described in the "Kalevala", the Finnish national epic. While its exact appearance and function are subject to interpretation, many believe it to be a magical artifact bringing wealth and prosperity to its owner. The Sampo's quest is central to many stories, where heroes try to possess or protect him.

Väinämöinen, the wise singer and central hero of the Kalevala, plays a crucial role in the history of the Sampo. In one of the stories, an epic battle is fought for control of this relic, which is eventually destroyed, scattering its wealth in all directions, thus bringing prosperity to Finland.

Next time you're immersed in Finnish literature, keep an eye out for this magical talisman. Sampo is a powerful symbol of wealth and aspiration, rooted in the Finnish cultural soul.

Fact 23 - The bear, a sacred animal of folklore

You've probably heard about the importance of the bear in various cultures, but do you know how sacred this animal is in Finnish folklore? The bear, or "karhu" in Finnish, is much more than just a mammal for Finns.

Historically, the indigenous peoples of Finland worshipped the bear as a spirit of the forest, a creature with mystical powers. They believed that the bear was the embodiment of their ancestors and treated it with the utmost respect. After a hunt, rituals were often performed to appease the bear's spirit and ensure a successful hunt the following year.

Many Finnish legends speak of the bear as heroic or protective. For example, in some stories, he helps humans in their quest, or serves as a guide through dense forests.

To this day, the bear holds a special place in the hearts of Finns. It is a source of inspiration for artists, writers and even athletes. When you're walking around Finland, keep your eyes peeled: the powerful imprint of this sacred animal is everywhere.

Fact 24 - The Magic of the Polar Night

Have you ever imagined a place where the sun doesn't rise for weeks? Welcome to Finland during the polar night! This phenomenon occurs every year in the Arctic region of Finland, especially in Lapland, where the sun remains hidden below the horizon.

It's not just an extended night. The polar night, or "kaamos" in Finnish, immerses you in a supernatural atmosphere. The sky takes on a deep bluish hue, creating an almost unreal landscape. Despite the absence of sunlight, a soft, diffuse light emanates from the sky, giving a magical touch to the snowy landscape.

But the polar night also offers another fascinating spectacle: the Northern Lights. These dancing lights that color the sky green, pink, purple or even red are a sight not to be missed. Lapland is one of the best places in the world to see this phenomenon.

If you have the opportunity to visit Finland during this time, get ready for an unforgettable experience. The magic of the polar night is one of those wonders that nature offers us.

Fact 25 - Kuksa, the traditional wooden cup

When you think of Finland, do you imagine a people in harmony with nature? The "kuksa" is perfect proof of this. This traditional mug, hand-carved from a gnarled piece of birch, is a treasure of Finnish heritage. It reflects simplicity, sustainability and respect for the environment.

Each kuksa is unique, bearing the marks of its creator and the tree from which it comes. The Sami, the indigenous people of Lapland, have a special tradition related to this cup: before using it for the first time, they baptize it by filling it with coffee, tea or even alcohol. This gives it a soul.

If you're lucky enough to own one, you should know that it requires special maintenance. Avoid detergents, preferring clear water to clean it. Over time, your kuksa will develop a beautiful patina, a testament to the moments shared.

So, kuksa is not just a simple cup. It is a symbol of a Finnish culture, way of life and a deep relationship with nature.

Fact 26 - The Legend of the Great Hero Väinämöinen

Immerse yourself in the epic world of Finnish mythology, and you'll meet the legendary Väinämöinen. This hero with magical powers is a central character in "Kalevala", Finland's national epic. With his melodious voice, he can charm animals, calm rough seas, and even influence the hearts of men.

Born from the waters even before the creation of the earth, Väinämöinen is often described as a sage, singer and magician. One of his most famous adventures sees him building a magical boat while singing, demonstrating the power of his songs. His quest for a wife, his rivalry with the young and impetuous Joukahainen, and his magical exploits form the heart of many of the stories of the "Kalevala".

If you travel to Finland, you'll see his influence everywhere. Numerous works of art, songs and cultural performances evoke this mythical hero and his place in Finnish national identity.

So, the next time you hear a Finnish melody, think of Väinämöinen and the magic of its nation-shaping songs.

Fact 27 - Thousands of Islands on the Coast

When you look at the Finnish coast, an impressive spectacle unfolds: thousands of islands stretch as far as the eye can see. Indeed, Finland has about 180,000 lakes and, just as amazingly, almost 40,000 islands. It is one of the most fragmented coastlines in the world, offering a diversity of breathtaking landscapes.

The Turku archipelago, for example, is a special jewel of this island complex. With nearly 20,000 islands and islets, it is one of the largest inland sea island regions in the world. During the summer, this place comes alive with residents and tourists looking to enjoy the natural beauty, waterfront saunas, and the Northern Lights.

Further north, the Kainuu Islands offer a wilder experience, with vast forests, peaceful lakes, and abundant wildlife. It's a paradise for outdoor enthusiasts, whether it's fishing, hiking, or just relaxing.

So, if you're looking for a unique island experience, Finland is definitely the destination for you. Its islands promise unforgettable memories.

Fact 28 - The Challenge of Swimming in the Ice

Imagine diving into icy waters, surrounded by a frozen expanse of snow. In Finland, it's not just a crazy idea, it's a tradition called "avantouinti" or swimming in the ice. Courage and adrenaline are the order of the day for those who embark on this adventure.

The process begins by carving a square hole in the thick ice of a frozen lake or river. Once this is done, the swimmers, dressed in swimsuits and often wearing hats, immerse themselves in the frigid water. For many, it's an invigorating experience that stimulates the body and mind, and is believed to have many health benefits.

Every year, Finland hosts the World Ice Swimming Championships, where participants from all over the world come to compete against the frozen waters. These competitions are as much a celebration of human bravery as they are of Finland's unique culture.

So, if you're feeling adventurous and looking for an unforgettable experience, why not try the challenge of ice swimming on your next visit to Finland?

Fact 29 - Why Finns Love Simplicity

When you delve into Finnish culture, you'll quickly notice a trend: simplicity is king. This is not a coincidence, but a reflection of a philosophy deeply rooted in the national soul. Finns value authenticity and minimalism, seeking to eliminate the unnecessary to focus on the essentials.

Finnish architecture and design are prime examples. Think of Alvar Aalto, a famous architect and designer, whose works fuse functionality with sleek aesthetics. His creations, such as the Savoy vase, demonstrate a search for harmony between man, object and nature.

This inclination for simplicity is also found in everyday life. Finns often prefer the tranquility of a lakeside cottage to the hustle and bustle of a big city. They find pleasure in small moments, such as a walk in the forest or a moment of reflection in the sauna.

In Finland, simplicity is not seen as an absence, but as a way of accessing a form of purity and authenticity. It offers a return to basics, a break from a world that is often too complex.

Fact 30 - The secret to well-being in Finland

Have you ever heard of Finnish happiness? Finland has been repeatedly voted as the happiest country in the world in the World Happiness Report. But what is the secret to their well-being?

First, nature plays an essential role. Finland, with its vast forests and numerous lakes, offers a peaceful setting for relaxation. The intimate relationship that Finns have with their natural environment, such as walks in the forest or swimming in lakes, helps them to disconnect and recharge.

Secondly, the country's social welfare system plays a major role. Thanks to quality education, accessible healthcare, and a strong social security system, Finns have a safety net that goes a long way toward giving them peace of mind.

Finally, the sauna. More than just a tradition, it is a real institution. This ritual, practiced regularly, offers a moment of physical and mental relaxation, strengthening the social bond between the participants.

All in all, the combination of nature, a strong support system and deep-rooted traditions shapes the unique well-being of Finns.

Fact 31 - Salmiakki, a salty treat

Have you ever wondered what Finns like to eat as treats? Let me introduce you to "salmiakki", a confection that you will find difficult to categorize as sweet or savory.

At first glance, salmiakki looks like an ordinary black candy. But once in the mouth, a salty and strong flavor emerges, thanks to the ammonium chloride, an ingredient that gives it its unique taste. For many, it's an acquired taste; Some love it from the first bite, while others take a while to appreciate it.

This treat is so popular in Finland that it's not limited to sweets. You can find this flavor in various products, such as ice cream, liqueurs, and even chips! For example, the liqueur "Salmiakkikossu" combines the strength of salmiakki with that of vodka, for a truly Finnish experience.

So, if you're in Finland or if you come across salmiakki elsewhere, dare to try it! It could well be that this salty treat will become your new addiction or, at least, a memorable taste experience.

Fact 32 - Finland, Ice Hockey Champions

When you think of sports in Finland, ice hockey is undoubtedly at the top of the list. Did you know that Finland is one of the most formidable nations in the sport in the world?

For decades, hockey has been ingrained in Finnish culture. From an early age, many Finns lace up their skates and practice the sport on the country's frozen lakes. These winter training sessions paid off: Finland won several gold medals at the Ice Hockey World Championships.

Finland's impact on hockey doesn't stop there. You've probably heard of a few Finnish players playing in the big leagues, like Teemu Selänne or Jari Kurri, who have left an indelible mark on hockey history.

So, next time you're watching a hockey game, keep an eye out for the Finnish players. Their talent and determination on the ice is a testament to the rich heritage of the sport in Finland.

Fact 33 - Lapland's Giant Mosquitoes

Ah, the Lapland! This region of northern Finland is renowned for its breathtaking landscapes, Northern Lights and... its giant mosquitoes! Yes, you heard that right.

During the summer months, especially in July, an army of mosquitoes takes over the forests and marshes of Lapland. Even if they are not really "giant", their size is larger than the mosquitoes that are usually found in Europe. And if you're wondering why there are so many of them, the answer is simple: stagnant marsh water is the perfect place to lay their eggs.

However, there is no need to be overly alarmed. Although they can be annoying, these mosquitoes are not dangerous and do not transmit diseases. But if you're planning a trip to Lapland in the summer, remember to pack a good repellent!

At the end of the day, despite these little flying pests, the beauty and magic of the Lapland more than makes up for this little annoyance. After all, every paradise has its snake, doesn't it?

Fact 34 - The Influence of Christianity on Culture

When we talk about Finland, we often think of its rich ancestral culture. But do you know how much of a vital role Christianity has played in shaping modern Finnish identity?

Introduced around the 12th century, Christianity gradually replaced the old pagan beliefs. With his arrival, wooden churches adorned with religious art flourished in the country, such as the Straging Church of Petäjävesi, a UNESCO World Heritage Site.

This religious change didn't just affect the architecture. Christian festivals have become major events, such as the celebration of St. John's Day (Juhannus) in the summer. Although the pagan roots of this holiday endure, it is also associated with the birth of John the Baptist.

Thus, although Finland cherishes its traditions and legends of yesteryear, Christianity has profoundly shaped its cultural, artistic and festive landscape. A harmonious fusion of old and new that makes Finnish culture so unique.

Fact 35 - The haunting melodies of the kantele

You may have never heard of the kantele, but this stringed instrument has been at the heart of Finnish musical culture for centuries. Typical of the country, its soft and melodious sounds can transport you through the legends of times gone by.

Originating in the Karelia region, the kantele is often associated with Väinämöinen, the epic hero of the "Kalevala". According to legend, he made the first kantele from the jaws of a giant pike. The instrument has a simple look, but the sounds it produces are haunting and reminiscent of the vast wilderness of Finland.

Nowadays, the kantele is not just a relic of the past. Finnish music schools continue to teach this instrument, and it is not uncommon to hear its melodies at traditional festivals or in modern recordings.

So, if you have the opportunity to listen to a piece of kantele, close your eyes. Let yourself be carried away by its chords that tell you about the history and soul of Finland.

Fact 36 - The Mysterious Creature of Lake Näsi

You've probably heard of the Loch Ness Monster in Scotland, but did you know that Finland has its own aquatic legend? The deep waters of Lake Näsi are home to a mysterious creature that awakens the imagination and curiosity of many Finns.

For decades, witnesses have claimed to have seen a strange shape moving on the surface or under the waters of the lake. These sightings are often described as unusual waves, shadows, or serpentine shapes. Photos and videos have even been taken, although their authenticity is often debated.

But what could be hiding in the depths of Lake Näsi? Scientists are skeptical about the existence of such a creature, suggesting instead natural phenomena or giant fish. Nevertheless, the legend lives on, fueled by tales and speculation.

Next time you're walking along Lake Näsi, keep your eyes peeled. Who knows? Maybe you'll be the next witness to this age-old Finnish mystery.

Fact 37 - The Brave Lemminkäinen and His Adventures

Have you ever heard of the Finnish hero Lemminkäinen? Hailing from the national epic "Kalevala", this young and daring adventurer is known for his exploits and his quest for love. His bravery is a source of inspiration for many Finnish tales and songs.

One of his most famous adventures is when he tries to seduce the beautiful Aino, but she chooses to turn into a fish to escape his advances. This tale depicts passion, grief and sacrifice, universal themes that still resonate today.

But Lemminkäinen is not just a seducer. He also faced off against the fearsome Tuli-Hisi, a fiery creature, in an epic fight to protect his land and people. These stories are a reminder of the bravery of Finnish warriors and their determination to protect their homeland.

On your next trip to Finland, immerse yourself in the tales of the "Kalevala" and discover the rich and fascinating legacy that Lemminkäinen left behind. These adventures will give you a deep insight into Finnish culture and identity.

Fact 38 - The Magic of Midsummer Fires

Imagine a night when the sun hardly sets, the light dances in the sky and Finland lights up with twinkling lights. Tonight is Midsummer, or "Juhannus" in Finnish, one of the most anticipated celebrations of the year.

Finns gather around large fires, called "kokko", which glow in the night. These fires symbolize purification, protection, and good luck. According to an old tradition, by jumping over fire, you can ward off evil spirits or even attract love.

But it's not just a fire party. People also gather around lakes, dancing, singing and enjoying the beauty of Finnish nature. For example, it is common to see floating flower crowns, tossed by young girls in the hope of predicting their future lover.

So, if you have the opportunity to experience a Midsummer in Finland, don't hesitate to join in the festivities. It's the perfect opportunity to immerse yourself in authentic Finnish tradition and feel the magic that surrounds it.

Fact 39 - Finns Ski World Champions

Have you ever watched a ski competition on TV and noticed the number of Finnish flags flying proudly? There's a reason for that. Finland, with its winter climate and snowy landscapes, has produced some of the world's most talented and renowned skiers.

Since the start of the Olympic Winter Games, Finland has amassed an impressive collection of medals in skiing. Names like Matti Nykänen, who won four Olympic gold medals in ski jumping, are etched in the history of the sport. His technique and talent were unmatched, making him a true legend.

But it's not just ski jumping. The Finns also excel in cross-country skiing, with athletes like three-time Olympic champion Marja-Liisa Kirvesniemi. His stamina and determination inspired a whole generation of Finnish skiers.

Next time you're watching a ski competition, keep an eye out for Finnish athletes. With their long history and passion for the sport, they are often the ones leading the race and captivating the world's attention.

Fact 40 - The secret of Finnish longevity

Have you ever wondered why so many Finns live long and healthy lives? The answer lies in a mix of cultural, environmental and dietary factors that make Finland a place for long life.

Firstly, the Finnish way of life is closely linked to nature. Whether it's walking, skiing or fishing, outdoor activities are ingrained in Finnish culture. These regular physical activities, combined with the clean air of Finland's forests, contribute greatly to heart and overall health.

Secondly, the Finnish diet, which is rich in fish, berries and whole grains, plays a key role. For example, regular consumption of salmon, which is rich in omega-3s, is associated with a reduction in heart disease. In addition, berries like lingonberries and arctic raspberries, often picked in the wild, are packed with antioxidants.

Finally, Finland attaches great importance to mental health and well-being. The concept of "sisu", this Finnish resilience and determination, as well as regular saunas, help Finns manage stress and stay mentally balanced. Embrace these secrets, and maybe you too can enjoy a longer and healthier life!

Fact 41 - The Art of Silent Conversation

Have you ever wondered: why do some Finns prefer silence to words? In many cultures, prolonged silence during a conversation can feel uncomfortable. But in Finland, it's a form of art and respect.

The value of silence in Finland goes back to its agricultural and rural roots. In the vast wilderness of the country, where neighbours can be miles apart, silence has become synonymous with peace and contemplation. A common example is the simple activity of standing silently by a lake, observing nature.

In conversation, Finns often consider silence to be golden. This means that when they speak, it's to add value to the conversation. It's not uncommon to see two Finns sit together, enjoy a quiet moment, and then exchange a few well-chosen words.

So, the next time you find yourself in a conversation with a Finn and there is silence, know that it's a sign of respect. It gives you the space to reflect and enjoy the moment. Embrace it.

Fact 42 - Why Are Shoes Left At The Door

If you visit a Finnish home, you will quickly notice a custom: leaving your shoes at the entrance. It's not just about hygiene, but it's deeply rooted in Finnish culture and etiquette.

In Finland, the seasons can be extreme. Winter brings snow and mud, while summer can see sudden rains. By leaving the shoes outside, Finns ensure that dirt and moisture stay out. For example, after a day of skiing or hiking, it's natural to leave your boots at the entrance to avoid getting the house dirty.

But beyond the practical aspect, it also has a symbolic connotation. Walking into a house without shoes is like entering a sacred space. It is a mark of respect for the host and his home. It's also a way to feel more comfortable, almost like entering a sanctuary.

The next time you're invited to a Finn's house, consider leaving your shoes at the door. This will show your respect and understanding for this beautiful tradition.

Fact 43 - Trolls Who Live Under the Mountains

Deep in Finland's wild landscapes lie ancient legends, and one of the most captivating is that of the trolls who live under the mountains. These mythical creatures are deeply rooted in Finnish folklore, and each mountain, valley or forest has its own story to tell.

Trolls are often described as stone giants, sometimes friendly, sometimes mischievous. It is said that when exposed to sunlight, they turn to stone, creating the unique rock formations found in Finland. If you're walking near Mount Pallas, for example, some strange shapes might just be petrified trolls!

These legends are not just stories to scare children. They have played a vital role in the way Finns perceive and respect nature. Trolls are considered guardians of the land, and their presence is a reminder of the importance of living in harmony with the environment.

So, the next time you're in Finland and exploring its vast wilderness, keep your eyes peeled. Who knows? Maybe you'll be lucky enough to come across a troll, or at least, feel its ancient and magical presence around you.

Fact 44 - The Power of the Wolf in Legends

The wolf, a mysterious and powerful creature, occupies a central place in Finnish folklore. Throughout the ages, it has been revered, feared, and often misunderstood. In the collective imagination, the wolf is not just a wild animal; it is a reflection of the hopes, fears and wisdom of Finns.

Ancient Finnish stories often tell of the relationship between man and wolf. In some, the wolf is a spiritual guide, leading lost souls through the dense forests. As an example, a legend tells of a young man saved from the dangers of winter by a majestic wolf who guides him to his village.

But the wolf is not always seen in a favorable light. Some legends speak of a cunning and deceitful animal, testing the cunning and courage of humans. These stories are often a reminder of the need to respect nature and its creatures, as they hold powers that cannot be ignored.

So, if you delve into Finnish fairy tales, you'll discover the rich web of emotions, lessons, and mutual respect that binds humans to wolves, making these animals much more than just wild beasts.

Fact 45 - The Log Cabin Tradition

Finland, with its vast pine and birch forests, is the birthplace of a unique architectural tradition: the log cabin. These rustic structures, deeply rooted in Finnish history, symbolize the intimate connection between Finns and their natural environment.

For centuries, log cabins have been built using traditional methods, passed down from generation to generation. Each log is carefully chosen, squared and stacked to create strong, insulating walls. A typical hut, such as the one in Petäjävesi, a UNESCO World Heritage village, is a testament to the craftsmanship and precision of Finnish craftsmen.

These cabins are not just historical monuments or tourist attractions. Many Finns continue to live, at least temporarily, in these homes. In winter, surrounded by snow, or in summer, by a glistening lake, these cabins offer a peaceful refuge from the hustle and bustle of modern life.

So, if you're heading to Finland, don't hesitate to experience a night in an authentic log cabin. You will discover a world where simplicity and nature reign supreme.

Fact 46 - How the Reindeer Helps Santa Claus

Ah, Santa Claus and his faithful reindeer! Did you know that legend closely links these majestic creatures to Finland? Indeed, it is in the land of a thousand lakes and forests that reindeer play a crucial role in the magic of Christmas.

Finnish Lapland, located in the north of the country, is often referred to as Santa's real home. Here, reindeer are not just legendary animals, but an integral part of Sami culture. These reindeer are well-trained and adapted to the Arctic environment. Thanks to their wide hooves, they move easily over snow and ice, making them the perfect travel companions for Santa on his world tour.

Every year, children around the world write letters to Santa, hoping that his flying reindeer, with their glittering magic, will bring gifts to their doorstep. Among them, Rudolph, the red-nosed reindeer, is the most famous, guiding the sleigh through the darkest nights.

So, the next time you spot a shooting star in the winter sky, think of these magical reindeer from Finnish Lapland, flying from one end of the world to the other to bring joy and happiness.

Fact 47 - The Beauty of Runic Songs

Have you ever heard the ancient melodies that travel through time, resonating with the wisdom and legends of a distant era? In Finland, these melodies take the form of runic songs, a precious heritage that continues to captivate hearts.

Runic songs, known as "runolaulu" in Finnish, are sung poems, punctuated by a particular cadence and often accompanied by the kantele, the national instrument. These songs tell stories of heroes, love, war and myths, being an essential part of Finnish folklore. One of the most famous examples is the "Kalevala", a national epic compiled by Elias Lönnrot in the 19th century from traditional songs.

These melodies are not only preserved as relics of the past. They live and breathe in modern festivals, performance arts and even schools, where young Finns learn to sing them with pride.

Next time you're in Finland, keep an ear open. Perhaps you will be lucky to hear these haunting songs, weaving the threads of a rich and profound history that unites the past with the present.

Fact 48 - The Role of Women in Mythology

Did you know that Finnish mythology gives an important place to female figures, endowed with powers, wisdom and courage? Far from being mere secondary characters, they are at the heart of many legends, symbolizing the strength and resilience of the Finnish people.

One of the most emblematic figures is Louhi, the witch of the North, present in the "Kalevala". Despite her reputation as an evil witch, she is also a protector of her people and a fearsome mother. Her magical powers and determination make her a formidable opponent for the heroes of the "Kalevala".

There's also Aino, a young woman who chooses freedom and nature over being married against her will. Her story is a hymn to independence and the power of female choice, even in the face of tradition.

Finnish legends remind us that women have always been, and continue to be, pillars of culture and national identity. Their stories, steeped in magic and mystery, still resonate today, inspiring new generations.

Fact 49 - The Strange Creature of Lake Inari

Have you ever heard of lake monster legends? Lake Inari, located in northern Finland, is home to mysterious stories that spark the imagination. This vast lake, enveloped by the wild beauty of Lapland, hides a well-kept secret within it.

According to ancient accounts, a creature, nicknamed "Inarijärvi", lives in the depths of these icy waters. Local fishermen reported seeing a gigantic shape, with glistening scales, moving beneath the surface. These ephemeral apparitions are often accompanied by unexplained waves, arousing both wonder and awe.

Testimonies dating back to the 19th century mention the encounter with this mystical being, describing a melodious, almost hypnotic sound, emanating from the depths when it is nearby. Some even say that the creature is a guardian of the lake, watching over its hidden treasures.

So, if one day you find yourself near Lake Inari, keep your ears open and keep your eyes open. Who knows? Maybe you'll be lucky enough to catch a glimpse of this marvel of Finnish folklore.

Fact 50 - Pyys, Sacred Birds of the North

Did you know that Finland is home to a species of bird that is considered sacred by indigenous peoples? These are the pyys, small, secretive birds that are of great importance in the culture of the Far North.

These birds, recognizable by their speckled plumage, are often associated with luck and protection. In ancient Finnish culture, it was believed that seeing a pyy was a positive omen, heralding good news or favorable change. Hunters, before an expedition, sought the blessing of the pyys to ensure the success of their quest.

Legends say that pyys were once messengers between humans and gods. They were able to carry the prayers of the faithful to heaven and bring back divine answers. Thus, their unique song was often seen as a message from the gods, and it was respected and honored.

The next time you're walking through the Finnish forests and hear a distinctive song, stop for a moment. You may well be in the presence of a pyy, the sacred bird that connects the world of men with that of the gods.

Fact 51 - Finland's invention of the smart card

Did you know that Finland is behind an innovation that has transformed the way we do our daily transactions? This is the smart card, the payment tool that is ubiquitous in our wallets today.

Indeed, although the smart card itself was conceptualized in France, it was in Finland that the first practical and consumer application of this technology was born. In the 1990s, the Finns pioneered the use of SIM cards in mobile phones, a development that was later adopted globally.

Thanks to this invention, mobile communication has become more secure and personalized. The ability to store information on a chip embedded in a card has revolutionized not only telecommunications, but also banking and many other industries.

So, the next time you insert your chip card to make a payment or put a SIM card in your phone, think about Finland. It is this Nordic country that has greatly contributed to making this technology a global standard.

Fact 52 - The Strange Mud Bath Ritual

Have you ever heard of a Finnish tradition that has its roots in antiquity and that might seem a bit unusual to you? I'm talking about the mud bath ritual in Finland.

In some parts of Finland, it is common to see people immersing themselves in peat marshes during the summer. This practice, which dates back centuries, is believed to have many benefits for the skin and overall health. The mineral properties of mud are said to purify the skin and improve blood circulation.

It's not just a beauty treatment, it's also a social experience. Families and friends often gather for these mud baths, turning this strange ritual into a moment of conviviality and relaxation.

So, if one day you find yourself in Finland during the warm season, why not give it a try? Indulge in this tradition, wrap yourself in mud and feel the blessings that Finns have cherished for generations.

Fact 53 - Cats of the Finnish Forest

Have you ever wondered where these beautiful cats with thick coats and bright eyes that you might meet in Finland come from? Well, they are the proud and wild descendants of Finnish forest cats.

These big cats, known locally as "Suomen Metsäkissa", have evolved to adapt to Finland's harsh environment. Their dense, lush coat protects them from the bitter cold of northern winters. As you observe these cats, you may notice their rugged gait and sharp claws, perfect for climbing trees and hunting.

It's not just their appearance that is remarkable, but also their character. These cats are known to be independent, but also incredibly loyal to those they consider their family. Many Finns will tell you stories of these faithful companions who followed them on long walks in the forest.

Next time you're out and about in a Finnish forest, keep an eye out. Who knows, you might come across one of these beautiful cats, giving you a glimpse of Finland's rich natural tapestry.

Fact 54 - Fairies Dancing in the Meadows

Have you ever heard the Finnish legends of fairies dancing in the meadows at nightfall? These enchanting beings, called "keijukainen" in Finnish, have been an integral part of Finnish folklore for generations.

These fairies, luminous and elusive, are often described as small winged creatures, illuminating fields and forests with their ethereal dances. On balmy summer nights, when the sky remains bright for long hours, Finns say that you can spot these creatures if you are quiet and patient.

But keijukainen are not only beings of beauty and light. They are also the guardians of meadows and forests, ensuring that nature remains intact and respected. According to popular belief, disturbing one of their dances could bring bad luck or bad luck.

So, if you ever find yourself in Finland during one of these magical nights, take a moment to sit back, listen, and observe. If you're lucky, you might witness one of nature's most mystical dances.

Fact 55 - The shortest day of the year

Did you know that Finland experiences a unique natural phenomenon during the winter? Located near the Arctic Circle, much of the country experiences what is known as the "kaamos", or the polar night period. During this time, the sun never really rises, resulting in the shortest day of the year.

This phenomenon occurs around the winter solstice, around December 21. In Utsjoki, for example, the sun almost completely disappears for almost 52 days. The sky is then adorned with bluish and pink hues, offering a spectacle of melancholic beauty.

But this is not a time of total darkness. The Northern Lights often light up the night sky, creating shimmering webs of light that dance through the darkness. These natural lights compensate for the absence of sunlight, making the Finnish winter magical.

So, while the idea of such short days may seem daunting, Finland has found a way to celebrate that darkness with its unique natural beauty. If you have the opportunity, this is a show not to be missed!

Fact 56 - The Mysteries of the Finnish Language

Have you ever heard of Finnish? This language, spoken mainly in Finland, is shrouded in mysteries and curiosities. Contrary to what one might think, Finnish is not related to Scandinavian languages, such as Swedish or Norwegian, but belongs to the Finno-Ugric language family.

One of the peculiarities of Finnish is its declination system. With its 15 grammatical cases, each noun can be modified to express different nuances, from place of origin to direction and much more. Let's take the word "kukka" (flower): "kukassa" means "in a flower" and "kukasta" means "of the flower".

Another fascinating feature is the presence of words that are "untraceable" in other languages. For example, the word "sisu" describes a determination and resilience specific to the Finnish character. There is no direct translation into other languages for this concept.

Finnish, although complex, is a melodious and rich language. If you're feeling adventurous, why not try to learn it? You will discover a linguistic world full of surprises!

Fact 57 - The Legend of the Winter Rainbow

Have you ever seen a rainbow in winter? In Finland, this natural phenomenon is not only rare, but it is also shrouded in a mythical aura. Ancient Finnish legends tell a captivating story about this.

According to tradition, the winter rainbow is the work of the goddess Lumikka, protector of snow. She would use it as a bridge to cross the sky during the colder months. When the rays of the low winter sun meet the fine ice particles in suspension, they create this colorful spectrum.

This phenomenon is so peculiar that the ancient Finns considered it an omen. If a winter rainbow was spotted, it was seen as a sign that Lumikka was satisfied and that the winter would be mild. On the other hand, his absence presaged a harsh winter.

The next time you're under the Finnish sky in winter, look up and look for that beautiful rainbow. Who knows, maybe Goddess Lumikka will smile at you from the heavens.

Fact 58 - The Ice Fishing Competition

Do you know the Finns' passion for ice fishing? When the lakes freeze over, the hobby becomes a national obsession. And that's not all: they've even turned it into a competition!

In Finland, the National Ice Fishing Championship is held every winter. Equipped with drills to punch holes in the ice, participants compete to catch the largest number or the biggest fish in a limited amount of time. A prominent example is Matti Virtanen, who won the championship in 2018 with an impressive catch in just a few hours.

But it's not just a question of competence. Ice fishing is also a moment of conviviality. Competitors exchange tips, tell stories and share unforgettable moments around a fire with a cup of hot chocolate in hand.

The next time you visit Finland in the winter, try to join this competition or, at least, observe the art of ice fishing. You will discover a fascinating facet of Finnish culture.

Fact 59 - How to Build a Finnish Igloo

Have you ever dreamed of sleeping in an igloo? In Finland, this is a reality, and the Finns have mastered the art of building these ice shelters. Here's how they do it, and you'll be surprised at how ingenious it is.

It all starts with the choice of snow. It must be compact and moist so that the cut blocks retain their shape. Eero, a Finnish expert in igloo construction, usually uses a saw to cut the blocks precisely, forming an upward spiral.

Next, it is crucial to tilt the blocks slightly inwards, creating a self-supporting structure. It also creates an insulating effect, keeping the inside of the igloo nice and warm, despite the freezing temperatures outside. Pekka, another enthusiast, says he spent a night outside at -20° C, while being comfortably ensnit inside his igloo.

If you travel to Finland during the winter, you might meet experts like Eero or Pekka. They will be able to show you how to erect your own igloo and give you a truly arctic experience.

Fact 60 - The Great Fire of the Autumnal Equinox

Every year at the autumnal equinox, the skies of Finland are illuminated not only by the Northern Lights, but also by an equally captivating earthly spectacle: the Great Fire. This ritual, deeply rooted in Finnish culture, has a history and meaning that you will find fascinating.

Originally, this blaze was lit to celebrate the end of summer and prepare for the arrival of the long winter. According to an old legend, Liisa, a woman from the village of Rovaniemi, was the first to initiate this tradition. She is said to have lit a huge fire to guide her husband lost in the darkness, symbolizing the light in the darkness.

Fire also has a spiritual significance. Many believe that the flames purify the soul and ward off evil spirits, preparing the inhabitants for the dark months ahead. For example, Joonas, an elder from Ivalo village, says fire helps him reconnect with his ancestors and honor their memory.

If you have the chance to visit Finland during this time, don't miss this ceremony. The brilliance of the great fire, combined with the mystical dance of the Northern Lights, is a truly magical experience.

Fact 61 - The Independence Day Feast

On 6 December, Finland celebrates its independence, a day marked by solemn commemorations, but also by joyful celebrations. And like any good Finnish event, Independence Day wouldn't be complete without a traditional feast to honor this special day.

Historically, the Independence Day feast evokes the resilience and ingenuity of the Finnish people. The menu often consists of local dishes such as gravlax salmon, game, and reindeer stew. You may be surprised to learn that the reindeer dish, once considered a subsistence food, has become a delicacy and sought-after, especially by the Korhonen family of Kuopio, who have been making it for generations.

This feast is also an opportunity for Finns to gather with family and friends. Candlelight, traditional songs, and sharing meals strengthen bonds and shared memories. The Laaksonen family from Turku, for example, has a tradition where each member tells what they value most about Finnish culture.

If you happen to be in Finland on this day, be sure to take part in this feast to taste the country's delicacies and immerse yourself in its rich traditions.

Fact 62 - The Treasure Hunt of Legends

Finland is a country rich in myths and legends, and one of the most captivating stories is about hunting for hidden treasures. For centuries, these tales have fascinated Finns, infusing them with a sense of adventure and mystery.

For example, the legend of Lemminkäinen, a hero of the Kalevala (the Finnish national epic), speaks of a treasure hidden in the heart of Finland, protected by ancient spells. It is said that only one who possesses a pure heart can access this treasure. Eero, a passionate treasure hunter from Helsinki, has spent years studying this legend, looking for clues in ancient manuscripts.

Finland's dense forests and shimmering lakes have often been the scene of daring quests. In 1987, a team led by Aino Mäki, a local adventurer, claimed to have discovered an ancient map leading to treasure near Lake Päijänne, fueling the treasure hunting craze.

If you're intrigued by the idea of hunting for legendary treasure, Finland is the perfect place to start your quest. Who knows, maybe you'll be the next to discover the hidden riches of this mysterious country?

Fact 63 - Finnish Children's Winter Games

In Finland, winter is much more than a cold season. For Finnish children, it's a huge playground. When the first snowflakes fall, a magical transformation takes place, transforming familiar landscapes into veritable winter playgrounds.

A particularly popular game is the "akankanto", literally "pine cone carrier". Children form teams and take turns to transport pine cones from one point to another as quickly as possible, often using sleds or simple wooden sleds. This game, which combines competition and cooperation, is played in schoolyards and parks across the country.

Another popular game is "lumilinna", which means "snow castle". Armed with shovels and buckets, the young Finns are busy building impressive fortresses and ephemeral sculptures. In 1996, in Kemi, a group of children even set a record by building the largest snow castle ever!

So, if you find yourself in Finland during the winter, don't hesitate to join these little architects and budding athletes. You will discover a simple joy, that of playing in the snow.

Fact 64 - The Miracle of the Singing Ice

Have you ever heard a melody emanating from the ice? In Finland, this strange and fascinating phenomenon is called "the ice that sings". When the conditions are right, Finland's frozen lakes offer an unforgettable natural concert.

This sound phenomenon occurs when thin layers of new ice interact with forces such as wind or currents. The vibrations caused cause the ice to resonate, producing sounds ranging from gentle ringing to deep rumblings. On Lake Inari, for example, you can witness this wonder during the first frost of the year.

Finnish researchers have studied this phenomenon and found that the sound quality of ice is affected by its temperature, thickness and salt content. The result is a range of sounds as varied as snowflake patterns.

If you ever find yourself near a frozen lake in Finland, keep your ears open. You might just be the lucky listener of one of the most exceptional concerts nature has to offer.

Fact 65 - The Enchanted Forests of the North

Here you are, entering the green immensity of the northern Finnish forests. These vast expanses of woodland are not just groupings of trees: they are steeped in legends, mysteries and ancient magic that Finns cherish deeply.

Every tree trunk, every moss under your feet has a story to tell. It is said that the spirits of the forest, the "metsänhenki", watch over these places, protecting animals and plants. If you walk near Lapland Forest at dusk, you might even spot will-o'-the-wisps, those ethereal glows dancing between the trees.

But these forests are not just the realm of the supernatural. They also provide valuable resources, such as wood, berries, and mushrooms. In August, for example, wild blueberries abound, offering a delicious harvest for those who know where to look.

On your next visit to Finland, don't forget to lose yourself for a while in these enchanting woods. Who knows what wonders you'll discover there?

Fact 66 - The Role of Stars in Folklore

Imagine lying on an icy expanse in Finland, the stars twinkling above you in the dark night. To you, these celestial lights are beautiful, but to Finns, they are much more than that: they are full of ancient stories and traditions.

The stars, for the Finnish people, have always been guides. In folklore, they were often seen as the souls of those who have left us, watching over the world of the living from heaven. The North Star, for example, is seen as a celestial compass, always showing the direction of the "koti," or house.

But it's not all calming stories. Finnish mythology also talks about the Milky Way, called "Linnunrata", which means "The Path of the Birds". According to legend, it was created when the cosmic bird flew towards the sun, leaving behind a trail of stardust.

The next time you look at the starry sky in Finland, remember the legends associated with it. Each star has its own story, rooted in the heart of Finnish culture.

Fact 67 - The Enigma of the Midnight Sun

Have you ever wondered what it would be like to live on a never-ending day? In Finland, this phenomenon is very real during the summer, especially north of the Arctic Circle. The midnight sun is not a legend, but a mesmerizing natural spectacle that leaves the skies bathed in golden light for days and nights in a row.

The phenomenon is due to the tilt of the Earth. During the summer, the North Pole is tilted toward the Sun, allowing the Arctic Circle to remain illuminated 24 hours a day. In Rovaniemi, for example, the sun doesn't set for almost 70 consecutive days in summer!

But it's not just an astronomical curiosity. For Finns, the midnight sun is also a time of celebration, activities and celebrations. There is a palpable energy, with festivals and gatherings to celebrate this unique phenomenon.

The next time you visit Finland in the summer, get ready to be dazzled by this celestial spectacle. It is an experience that recalls the magic of our world, a wonder not to be missed.

Fact 68 - The Story of the First Finnish School

Do you know the history of the first school in Finland? It's a story that goes back to the Middle Ages, a time when education was a rare privilege. Turku, Finland's oldest city, is the birthplace of this educational revolution.

In the 13th century, Turku Cathedral founded the country's first school. Intended primarily to train priests, this institution was primarily religious. However, it laid the foundation for what would later become a world-renowned education system. Ancient manuscripts testify to the teaching of Latin, theology and philosophy.

This was just the beginning. Over the centuries, Finland has understood the importance of education for all. Today, the country is famous for its progressive and egalitarian education system. But it all started with this humble school in Turku.

Next time you visit Turku, take a moment to reminisce about this history. Every stone, every street, carries with it the echoes of a past dedicated to the quest for knowledge.

Fact 69 - Why Fish Is So Precious

You're probably wondering why Finns love fish so much. Let me plunge you into the depths of this intimate relationship. Finland, with its thousands of lakes, has always had a natural connection with fishing, making it central to its culture and economy.

Since prehistoric times, people have been drawing on fresh water to feed their families. Fish, especially herring and salmon, were an essential source of protein. Even today, some villages perpetuate ancestral fishing techniques, such as wicker traps or trout nets.

Then there is the economic dimension. Over the centuries, the fish trade shaped the development of several Finnish cities. Pori, for example, became wealthy thanks to its active port where the precious herring transited.

So, whenever you enjoy a fish dish in Finland, remember that it is not only a delicacy, but also a piece of history. A cultural and economic heritage that has endured through the ages.

Fact 70 - The Day Finland Stopped Time

Have you ever heard of the day Finland literally stopped time? It's a fascinating story that illustrates Finnish ingenuity in the face of a daunting challenge. It was 1921, and Finland, in its quest for modernity, wanted to synchronize its clock with that of its European neighbors.

At the time, Helsinki had an offset of 1:27 from the Greenwich meridian. To close this gap, the government decided to add 33 minutes to the Finnish clock. But instead of an abrupt transition, an ingenious method was adopted: for 11 consecutive days, each day, three minutes were added to official time.

This meant that during those 11 days, when the clocks showed midnight in Finland, it was actually only 11:57 p.m. The Finns, with their typical sense of rigour, have adapted brilliantly. Trains, schools and businesses have adjusted their schedules accordingly.

Thus, this small time adjustment has become an emblematic example of how Finland, despite the obstacles, remains committed to modernizing and connecting with the rest of the world.

Fact 71 - The Magical Power of Stones

Did you know that Finland is the birthplace of many ancient legends related to stones? These ancestral stories tell of supernatural powers attributed to certain stones, often found in the country's mystical forests and lakes.

It is said that the stones, shaped by time and the elements, carry within them the energy of the Earth itself. For example, in some areas, a rounded stone found by a lake is considered to bring good luck and protection. Some ancients wore it as a talisman to ward off evil spirits.

Finnish shamans, or "noaidi", also used these stones in rituals and ceremonies. They believed that these objects, when used correctly, could guide souls, cure diseases, or even predict the future. A famous example is the "Karsikko", an engraved stone used to commemorate the deceased and protect the living.

These ancestral beliefs and practices, while largely forgotten, remain etched in Finnish culture. So, on your next walk in Finland, keep your eyes peeled: you might just stumble upon a magic stone!

Fact 72 - The Dance of the Will-o'-the-Wisps

Have you ever heard of will-o'-the-wisps? Those mysterious glimmers that suddenly appear in swamps and wetlands? Finland, with its vast expanses of wetlands, is a favorite place for this enigmatic phenomenon, shrouded in legends and mysteries.

The ancient Finns believed that these lights were the spirits of the dead, seeking to guide the living or lead them astray. In some stories, they are associated with hidden treasures, leading those who follow them to priceless riches. For example, it is said that a fisherman, attracted by these lights, discovered a pot of gold hidden in a swamp.

However, science has a more down-to-earth explanation. These lights are caused by the combustion of gases emitted by the decomposition of organic matter in waterlogged soils. This natural phenomenon is known as "marsh phosphorescence".

But even with this scientific explanation, the will-o'-the-wisp dance remains a fascinating and mystical spectacle. If you're lucky enough to see them on a calm night in Finland, you'll surely get swept away by their ancient magic.

Fact 73 - The Mystery of the Northern Swamps

Speaking of marshes, did you know that Finland is home to some of the most mystical and unspoilt marshes in Europe? These wetlands, covered with moss and peat, stretch as far as the eye can see, offering a unique and mesmerizing landscape, especially under the bright summer sky of the north.

Historically, Finnish marshes were often considered sacred places. Some believed that these grounds were inhabited by spirits and supernatural creatures. For example, an old legend tells the story of a shepherd who, while playing his flute in a swamp, attracted a water nymph who danced for him all night.

These vast expanses are also of major ecological importance. They serve as habitat for a variety of animal and plant species, some of which are endemic to the region. Wolves, brown bears and capercaillie are just a few examples of animals that find refuge in these wetlands.

So, if you ever find yourself exploring these mysterious swamps, take a moment to feel the ancient energy that permeates these places. Who knows, maybe you'll have an unexpected encounter with a creature from legends?

Fact 74 - The Journey of Migratory Birds

Did you know that every year Finland becomes a major crossroads for thousands of migratory birds? This natural spectacle is both fascinating and vital to the local ecosystem. As spring sets in, the Finnish sky comes alive with the incessant ballet of these birds heading north.

Many birds, such as cranes, whooper swans, and sandpipers, choose Finland's lakes, marshes, and shorelines as temporary stopovers. For example, Liminka Bay National Park is one of the most popular lookout points. There, you can see thousands of birds congregating, feeding, and resting before continuing their long journey.

But why Finland? It provides a rich and preserved habitat, crucial for the survival of these birds during their migration. The country's geographical position, at the crossroads between East and West, also makes it an essential place to visit.

So, the next time you look up at the Finnish sky in the spring, remember the incredible journey these birds are embarking on and the importance of Finland's role in their journey.

Fact 75 - The Soothing Sounds of Nature

Have you ever closed your eyes and simply listened to the gentle whisper of nature? In Finland, this experience becomes a symphony. Finland's forests, with their vast expanses of pine, birch and lakes, offer a unique melody that you won't find anywhere else.

Take, for example, the serene resonance of an icy stream meandering through the forest. Or the subtle crunch of the snow under your feet on a winter walk. These sounds are amplified by the deep silence that envelops the Finnish wilderness, allowing you to commune with nature.

But that's not all. In summer, you will be lulled by the melodious song of birds, the buzzing of insects and the gentle sound of the wind through the trees. Koli National Park, for example, is a place where these sounds create an almost meditative atmosphere.

So, next time you're visiting Finland, take a moment to sit back, breathe, and just listen. Finnish nature will speak to you in unexpected ways, offering peace of mind rarely found elsewhere.

Fact 76 - The Legend of the Mother of the Forest

Have you ever wondered why Finnish forests seem so mystical and alive? According to an ancient Finnish legend, all this is the work of the "Metsänemo", or "mother of the forest". She watches over every tree, every animal, guaranteeing the harmony and balance of these wild spaces.

The Metsänemo is often described as an elegant woman, wearing a bright green dress, with hair as long and lush as forest mosses. A famous example of this legend can be found in the folktales of the Karelia region, where it appears to guide and protect lost travelers.

But its role is not limited to protection. It also teaches respect for nature. Finns believe that displeasing the Metsänemo, such as cutting down trees for no reason or harming wildlife, can lead to its anger and misfortune.

So, on your next walk through the Finnish woods, take a moment to feel the presence of the Metsänemo. And remember to always treat your home, the forest, with the utmost respect.

Fact 77 - The Healing Power of Plants

Did you know that Finland is home to a multitude of plants with impressive medicinal properties? For generations, Finns have exploited the richness of their local flora to heal and alleviate various ailments. Their in-depth knowledge comes from ancestral traditions and careful observation of nature.

Take, for example, wild chamomile, often found in Finnish grasslands. It is renowned for its soothing properties, used in herbal tea to calm the nerves and promote sleep. Or arnica, which grows in mountainous regions, known to treat bruises and reduce inflammation.

Birch bark, an emblematic tree of Finland, is also proving beneficial. It is made into a decoction to detoxify the body and strengthen the immune system. Not to mention lingonberry berries, rich in antioxidants, often recommended for their preventive action against certain diseases.

Next time you visit Finland, don't hesitate to explore the forests and meadows. Maybe you'll discover the healing secrets that Finnish nature has to offer.

Fact 78 - The Tradition of Cradle Songs

Have you ever heard of the soft, soothing melodies that lull Finnish children to dreamland? For centuries, Finland has maintained a rich tradition of cradle songs, passed down from generation to generation. These songs reflect the parents' love, hope, and dreams for their offspring.

One of the most famous songs is called "Tuuti, tuuti, pieni poikanen", which can be translated as "Sleep, sleep, little boy". This sweet melody speaks of maternal protection and the beauty of the world that awaits the child. It has been sung by Finnish mothers for decades, if not longer.

In addition to their melodic beauty, these songs often have an educational role. They introduce children to the Finnish language, its musicality and rhythms. The lyrics, often inspired by nature and everyday life, evoke vivid and poetic images.

Next time you're in Finland, listen to the sweet melodies that waft through the air, especially at night. You might just witness this timeless musical tradition.

Fact 79 - The Magic of Winter's Tales

Have you ever felt the magic of a winter's night, where the snow covers everything with a white blanket and the world seems to be suspended in hushed silence? In Finland, this winter atmosphere has given rise to many tales and legends that have charmed generations of children and adults.

A folk tale tells the story of a little girl named Lumi, who, on a winter's night, befriends a star that has fallen from the sky. Together, they set out to discover the hidden wonders of the snowy forest, encountering fantastical creatures such as the silver fox and the luminescent owl.

These stories are not just entertainment. They impart life lessons, teaching perseverance, courage, and the importance of family and friendship. Finnish fairy tales are both mystical and deeply rooted in the reality of life in Finland.

The next time you're snuggling up on a cold winter's night, think of these Finnish tales and let yourself be swept away by their magic, because they have the power to light up even the darkest night.

Fact 80 - The Secrets of Lake Saimaa

Have you ever heard of Lake Saimaa, the jewel set in the heart of Finland? It is the largest lake in the country and holds many mysteries that have fueled legends and tales for centuries. Its deep waters and multiple islands hide secrets that only the lake knows.

One of these secrets is the Lake Saimaa seal, an endemic species that lives only in these waters. Despite the challenges posed by climatic conditions and human activities, this seal survived, making it a symbol of perseverance and resilience. His sighting is a rare and precious moment for those lucky enough to meet him.

But the lake isn't just home to amazing creatures. It has been the scene of many historical events. Archaeological remains suggest that its shores have been inhabited for millennia. From ancient canoes to fishing artifacts, each find tells a part of Finnish history.

Next time you're exploring Finland, don't forget to stop by Lake Saimaa. Let yourself be enveloped by its beauty and mysteries, and perhaps you will discover one of its many secrets.

Fact 81 - The Ice Circle Phenomenon

Have you ever wondered what wonders nature can create in winter? In Finland, the intense cold and freezing waters offer a breathtaking spectacle: the ice circles. These circular formations, slowly spinning on the water, seem to come straight out of a fairy tale.

Ice circles usually form in slow-moving rivers or lakes. When chunks of ice are swept away by the current and collide, they begin to rotate in a circle, gradually creating these circular structures through friction. The phenomenon is as fascinating as it is mysterious.

One of the most famous ice circles was observed on the Pite River in 2014. With a diameter of almost 50 meters, it rotated slowly, capturing the imagination of all who saw it. Videos of this phenomenon have gone around the world, highlighting the magic of Finnish nature.

If you're traveling to Finland during the winter, keep an eye out for these amazing trainings. They are a reminder of nature's ability to surprise and amaze us, even in the coldest conditions.

Fact 82 - The Reindeer's Journey to the South

When we think of Finland, we often think of reindeer. But did you know that these majestic creatures aren't just limited to the Arctic Circle? Every year, a fascinating phenomenon occurs: the reindeer's journey south.

Reindeer, which are usually associated with the northernmost regions of Finland, undertake an annual migration in search of food during the winter months. This quest sometimes takes them far beyond their traditional habitats, taking them through varied terrain and climates. It's an incredible journey, where the reindeer's stamina and determination are put to the test.

A remarkable example of this migration was observed in 2017, when a reindeer was spotted near the city of Tampere, several hundred kilometres from its usual habitat. This lonely journey captured national attention, illustrating the resilience of these creatures in the face of winter challenges.

If you're lucky enough to be in Finland during this time, keep your eyes peeled. You could witness this natural spectacle, a reminder of the amazing adaptability of the animal world.

Fact 83 - The Singing of the Trees in the Wind

Have you ever taken the time to stop in a Finnish forest and listen carefully? If so, you've probably witnessed this fascinating natural phenomenon: the melodious song of the trees as the wind blows through their branches.

In Finland, dense forests and majestic trees, such as spruce and pine, create a natural orchestra. When the wind blows, the branches rub against each other, producing a whistling melody that echoes through the woods. This soothing music is often described as a conversation between the trees, a harmonious dance of nature.

In 2019, a Finnish musician, Eero Aalto, even recorded these sounds during a light breeze in the Kainuu region. He used these recordings to compose a symphony, capturing the very essence of the Finnish forest in his music.

Next time you're in Finland, I invite you to take a walk in the forest, close your eyes and listen. You will be enveloped by this natural melody, a truly Finnish experience.

Fact 84 - The Magic of Shimmering Snow

Have you ever found yourself in a Finnish forest in winter, when daylight meets the surface of freshly fallen snow? If so, you've definitely noticed how each snowflake catches the light, creating a shimmering carpet as far as the eye can see.

This brilliance is no coincidence. In Finland, cold and wet weather conditions often produce crystal clear snow. The crystals in this snow reflect light from the sun, stars, and even the Northern Lights, giving the impression that the snow is encrusted with millions of diamonds.

This phenomenon has inspired many Finnish artists and writers. For example, renowned author Aila Meriluoto described in one of her poems the beauty of snowy forests under a starry sky, where each snowflake resembles a star that has fallen from the sky.

So, if you're lucky enough to travel to Finland in winter, don't forget to look for this light show. This is one of the many gifts that the Finnish winter offers to those who take the time to observe it.

Fact 85 - The History of the First Library

Delving into the history of Finland will inevitably lead you to a fascinating chapter: the creation of its first library. Did you know that Finland, despite its harsh climate and vast forests, became one of the first countries to value the sharing of knowledge through the library system?

The first Finnish library was established in Turku at the beginning of the 19th century. At that time, the importance of education and reading was already strongly rooted in Finnish culture. Inspired by the European educational movements, this library was much more than just a place to store books. It has become a symbol of progress and equality.

Personalities such as Elias Lönnrot, the eminent collector of the Kalevala, frequented this library. Their quest for knowledge and culture was facilitated by access to a vast collection of precious manuscripts and texts.

Today, every Finnish city boasts of having a library, a reminder of the importance the country places on knowledge and learning. And it all started with this humble institution in Turku.

Fact 86 - The Legend of the Lake Dragon

Have you ever heard of the mysterious Finnish legend of the lake dragon? It is a story that has stood the test of time, told from generation to generation, evoking the depths of Finland's crystal clear lakes.

According to legend, centuries ago, a majestic dragon lived in the depths of Lake Pielinen. With scales shining like mirrors and eyes that shone like stars, he ruled over the waters and the creatures that lived in them. He was a benevolent being, but formidable to those who wished him harm.

One day, a brave fisherman, Tapani, having heard of the treasures guarded by the dragon, decided to dive into the depths to find them. Instead, he met the dragon and, after a memorable conversation, learned the importance of respecting nature.

Today, even though the dragon has not been seen in centuries, locals believe that it still watches over the lakes. Each ripple, a murmur of water, is a reminder of his presence and the magic of Finnish legends.

Fact 87 - The Role of Elders in Culture

Do you know how precious seniors are in Finnish culture? Their role goes far beyond mere family figures; They are the custodians of the country's history, wisdom and traditions.

In Finland, elders are respected not only for their life experience, but also for their knowledge of ancestral traditions. They are often consulted in important family decisions and play a vital role in traditional ceremonies. For example, at a wedding, it is often the grandparents who pass on ancient rites and blessings.

Their influence doesn't stop there. Elders also play a crucial role in passing down folktales, songs, and recipes from generation to generation. Fireside vigils where grandparents tell stories of yesteryear are special moments that strengthen family bonds.

Finally, by acknowledging the value of seniors, Finland highlights the importance of intergenerational learning. Finnish culture is a reminder that the wisdom and knowledge of the elders are priceless treasures that must be cherished and preserved.

Fact 88 - The Mystery of the Song of the Earth

Have you ever stopped to listen to the silent song of the earth? In Finland, this strange and mysterious natural phenomenon is particularly felt, and it carries with it a fascinating history.

In remote areas of Finland, especially on quiet nights, some have reported hearing a faint and constant hum, similar to a distant song. This sound, often referred to as "the song of the earth", has no obvious source and has long been the subject of much speculation and legend.

The ancients say that this song is the soul of the earth itself communicating with its inhabitants. They believe that this sound contains echoes of centuries past, and by listening to it carefully, one could hear the voices of our ancestors. It's a testament to the deep connection between the land and Finns.

Although science cannot yet fully explain this phenomenon, the mysterious song of the earth remains an integral part of Finland's cultural heritage. It is an invitation to contemplation, respect for nature and recognition of our place in the universe.

Fact 89 - The Strange Tradition of Snow Bathing

Imagine stepping out of a hot sauna and diving straight into a stretch of fresh snow. If this seems inconceivable, know that it is a well-established tradition in Finland, practiced for centuries and recognized for its health benefits.

After a sauna session, the Finns, armed with courage, throw themselves into the snow, allowing their bodies to experience a thermal shock. This act, although surprising, is believed to stimulate blood circulation, strengthen the immune system, and provide a feeling of well-being and revitalization.

The example of the city of Rovaniemi, located in Lapland, is striking. Every winter, its inhabitants organize an event where hundreds of people, after enjoying the warmth of the sauna, lie together in the snow, forming a picture as surprising as it is hilarious.

If the idea of a snow bath seems too daring to you, remember that this tradition is a perfect illustration of the intimate relationship Finns have with nature, embracing its extremes with joy and respect.

Fact 90 - The Secret of Finnish Strength

Have you ever heard of the Finnish concept of "sisu"? It's much more than just a word; it embodies an essential part of Finland's national identity. "Sisu" describes unwavering determination, resilience in the face of adversity, and an iron will to overcome any obstacle.

This trait is reflected in many aspects of Finnish history. Take, for example, the Winter War, where Finland, despite being outnumbered, resisted the Soviet invasion with fierce determination. The mental and physical strength of Finnish soldiers, fueled by their "sisu", became legendary.

But it's not just in dramatic moments that the "sisu" manifests itself. In everyday life, Finns use this inner strength to face harsh winters, work hard, and maintain a deep sense of community. It is not uncommon to hear a Finn say that he has accomplished a difficult task thanks to his "sisu".

The next time you're faced with a challenge, remember the Finnish "sisu". Maybe that inner strength is also dormant within you, ready to be awakened.

Fact 91 - Shadows Dancing Under the Moon

Have you ever seen the sky come alive with a mystical dance on a clear night in Finland? These luminous shadows swaying and undulating in the sky are the Northern Lights, a natural phenomenon that has fascinated and amazed for millennia.

They are particularly visible in northern Finland, in Lapland. On a cloudless night, when darkness envelops the snowy landscape, you can witness these lights dancing in harmony with the moonlight. These Northern Lights have given rise to many Sami legends, such as that of the spirits playing football with the skull of a reindeer in the sky.

But it's not all magic and legends. These lights come from solar particles that collide with molecules in the Earth's atmosphere. The science behind this show is as fascinating as the show itself.

So, if you have the chance to visit Finland during the winter months, don't forget to look up at the sky. Maybe you'll be greeted by this luminous dance, a gift from nature itself.

Fact 92 - The Guardian Spirits of the House

As you walk through the Finnish countryside, you might notice small wood or stone carvings nestled near the entrances to houses. These statuettes are not mere ornaments: they represent the "haltija", protective spirits of the house.

These benevolent entities, derived from ancestral Finnish beliefs, are believed to watch over the inhabitants of the house and protect them from misfortunes. It is common for locals to give them gifts, such as food or drinks, as a sign of respect and gratitude. At Juhannus, the summer solstice festival, some Finns even leave a plate of food outside for their haltija.

There is a golden rule: never offend or neglect these protective spirits. There are stories circulating about people who ignored this tradition and suffered misfortunes or misfortunes as a result.

Next time you're in Finland, keep an eye out for these little statuettes. They are the living symbol of a tradition that combines respect for nature, ancestral beliefs and gratitude for the invisible forces that surround us.

Fact 93 - The Dance of the Fireflies in Summer

Summer in Finland is a magical time, where the days stretch almost endlessly. But when night finally begins to fall, another spectacle awaits you: the glittering dance of the fireflies. These small insects, which emit a soft light, transform Finnish forests into fairy tales.

It is fascinating to know that this glow, produced by a chemical reaction in the abdomen of fireflies, is actually courtship. These little creatures use their light to attract a mate and mate. Each species has its own blinking rhythm, which allows fireflies to find a mate of the same species.

If you find yourself in Finland during the summer, find a quiet spot away from the city lights. Lie down on the grass and let yourself be lulled by this luminous ballet. It's a moment of pure serenity, a communion with nature that you'll never forget.

Finland is full of wonders, and the Firefly Dance is one of the most memorable. A reminder that even in the dark, there is always a glimmer of hope.

Fact 94 - The Ancient Art of Finnish Weaving

Weaving has been a central part of Finnish culture for centuries. This ancestral art, passed down from generation to generation, testifies to the richness and complexity of Finland's heritage. If you dig through the treasures of a Finnish house, you're likely to discover hand-woven textiles, reflecting the family's history and identity.

Traditional motifs, such as geometric shapes and depictions of nature, tell stories. Each design has a meaning, often related to myths, legends, or historical events in the country. For example, the "Kalevala" pattern, inspired by the Finnish national epic, is a living testament to the importance of weaving in cultural storytelling.

Even today, many people practice this art with passion. If you're visiting Finland, take the time to attend a weaving workshop. You will be amazed by the dexterity and precision of the craftsmen, who transform simple threads into works of art.

The art of Finnish weaving is much more than just a textile technique. It is a window into the soul of a people, a link between the past and the present, a profound expression of national identity.

Fact 95 - The Beauty of Nature's Ballet

Finland is often described as the theatre where nature dances. In each season, you can witness a natural ballet, where each element plays an essential role in this ephemeral performance. In summer, for example, the midnight sun twirls the shadows and tints the lakes with a golden light, creating a stage worthy of the greatest spectacles.

In autumn, Finland's forests turn into a sea of colour. The red, orange and gold leaves dance in the wind, providing a stunning visual spectacle. This change of scenery heralds the winter ballet, where the snow covers everything with a blanket of white, and the Northern Lights light up the night sky, moving to the rhythm of silent music.

Spring, on the other hand, is the time of rebirth. Thawed lakes sparkle in the sun's rays, and wildlife awakens, adding life to this seasonal dance. Birdsong accompanies the budding of the trees, completing the ballet.

Every visit to Finland allows you to be a privileged spectator of this natural performance. It is an invitation to marvel at the ephemeral and renewed beauty of nature's ballet.

Fact 96 - The Legend of the Guardians of the Forest

Have you ever heard of the mysterious guardians of Finland's forests? According to an ancient legend, these protective spirits watch over the woods and everything that lives in them. They are described as ethereal figures, often invisible, but whose presence is felt by those who are in harmony with nature.

These guardians are tasked with protecting animals and plants from threats. It is said that when loggers cut down trees disrespectfully, or hunters take more than they need, the keepers step in. For example, some report being led astray by a sudden fog or hearing whispers that dissuaded them from continuing their actions.

In Finland, respecting the forest also means honouring these spirits. Many families teach their children to leave an offering, such as a piece of bread or a coin, as a sign of gratitude for the blessings of the forest.

These legends are more than just stories. They emphasize the importance of respect for nature and strengthen the deep connection between Finns and their ancestral forests.

Fact 97 - The Riddle of the Upside Down River

Have you ever imagined a river flowing upside down? In Finland, this astonishing phenomenon exists, and it intrigues locals and scientists alike. This is not just a legend; this is the Kutujoki River, located in the north of the country.

During the summer, due to a unique mix of melting ice, geology and topography, the water in the Kutujoki River appears to flow upside down for several days. This is not due to a real reversal of the current, but to an illusion created by the convergence of different streams of water at varying speeds. This show attracts many curious people every year.

The elders of the nearby village say that this phenomenon is the result of magic or an ancient blessing. For them, it's a reminder of Finland's unpredictable and wonderful nature.

The Kutujoki River is further proof of the richness and diversity of Finland's landscape. If you have the opportunity to visit it, don't forget to stop by and admire this unique spectacle in the world.

Fact 98 - Rituals of Transition from Childhood to Adulthood

Do you remember your transition to adulthood? In Finland, this transition is marked by traditional rituals that reinforce a sense of community and identity. Every stage of life is celebrated, and coming of age is no exception.

One of the most emblematic rites is the "Luistelu", where teenagers skate on the ice carrying a torch. At midnight, the torch is extinguished, symbolizing the end of childhood. As the sun rises, a new flame is lit, marking the beginning of their adult lives. This ceremony takes place in the tranquility of the Finnish night, surrounded by nature.

In addition to the "Luistelu", there is also the "First Fishing" ceremony. The teenager must catch his first fish alone, without help, thus showing his ability to support himself.

These rituals strengthen the bond between the individual and the community, and remind everyone of the importance of maturity and the responsibilities that come with adulthood.

Fact 99 - The Magic of the First Snows

Have you ever felt the excitement of the first snow? In Finland, this moment is awaited with impatience mixed with reverence. The first snowflakes that fall from the sky mark not only the beginning of winter, but also a spiritual renewal for many.

In Helsinki, for example, the first snow transforms the city into a fairytale landscape. The streets, parks and rooftops are adorned with a shimmering white coat, providing a striking contrast to the colourful facades of the buildings. Kids, bundled up in their wetsuits, set off to build the first snowman of the season, their laughter echoing through the fresh air.

In more rural areas, the first snowfall is also synonymous with preparation. Locals know it's time to stock up on wood for the long winter nights and check the insulation of their homes.

But beyond the practical aspects, the first snow is a moment of contemplation. It is a reminder of the ephemeral beauty of nature and encourages you to take a moment to appreciate the silent but dazzling spectacle it offers.

Fact 100 - The Story of Finland's First Winter

Have you ever wondered what the first winters were like in this faraway land? Let's go back to a time when Finland was still an unexplored land, swept by icy winds from the north.

Thousands of years ago, the first inhabitants of what is now Finland had to face a harsh and unforgiving winter, without modern technology. Armed only with their determination, they learned to hunt, fish and take refuge in makeshift shelters to survive the freezing temperatures. Artifacts found, such as stone tools and bones, testify to their ingenuity in the face of the challenges imposed by nature.

These ancestors also learned to respect the land, understanding the signs of nature and adapting their lifestyles to the seasons. Their traditions and knowledge have been passed down from generation to generation, shaping the Finnish culture we know today.

It is thanks to this ancestral history, made up of perseverance and respect for nature, that Finland has been able to develop such a special relationship with winter, celebrating it as a special moment rather than an obstacle to be overcome.

Conclusion

Here you are at the end of this incredible journey through the mysteries, legends and wonders of Finland. Together, we explored amazing facts, touching stories, and traditions that are deeply rooted in the fabric of this northern country. Hopefully, each page has brought you a new perspective, a new appreciation, or, at least, a renewed curiosity for this land of contrasts.

Finland, as you've discovered, is much more than saunas and the Northern Lights. It is a country rich in culture, history and nature, where each season, each region and each person has its own story to tell. Maybe you now feel inspired to visit this land, meet its people, or deepen your knowledge of its traditions?

Anyway, thank you for joining me on this journey. Finland is a country that, once discovered, never really leaves you. Keep these facts and stories in your heart, and who knows? Maybe one day, life's winding paths will lead you to those enchanting forests, peaceful lakes, and starry skies.

Have a wonderful day, dear reader, and remember that the world is filled with incredible facts waiting to be discovered. See you on your next adventure!

Marc Dresgui

Quiz

1) Where does the floor sing when touched?

   a) Beaches of Helsinki
   b) Lapland Mountains
   c) Forests of Western Finland
   d) Korouoma Marshes

2) What is the mythical animal that is supposed to inhabit Finnish lakes?

   a) Dragon
   b) Unicorn
   c) Kraken
   d) Phoenix

3) What activity do Finns like to immerse themselves in despite freezing temperatures?

   a) Alpine skiing
   b) Snow bath
   c) Diving
   d) Mountaineering

4) Who are considered the traditional custodians of Finnish houses?

   a) Elves
   b) Trolls

    c) Guardian Spirits
    d) Ogres

5) What natural phenomenon is nicknamed "the dance of the fireflies in summer"?

    a) Aurora borealis
    b) Shooting Stars
    c) Marine Bioluminescence
    d) Firefly Burst

6) What is the importance of elders in Finnish culture?

    a) They are knowledge keepers.
    b) They are the main tribal leaders.
    c) They predict the future.
    d) They run the government.

7) What are traditional Finnish textiles made of?

    a) Leather
    b) Recycled plastic
    c) Wool
    d) Cotton

8) What does snow look like when it sparkles in the Finnish sun?

    a) To emerald shards

- b) To Rain Pearls
- c) To diamonds
- d) To gold flakes

9) Which river is known to have the peculiarity of flowing upside down?

- a) Tammerkoski River
- b) Oulujoki River
- c) Kemijoki River
- d) Suttesaja River

10) Which legend is related to the protection of Finnish forests?

- a) Guardians of the Forest
- b) Wood Fairies
- c) Witches of the Forest
- d) Tree Nymphs

11) What is the highly respected ancient art in Finland?

- a) Wood carving
- b) Weaving
- c) Painting on canvas
- d) Ceramics

12) How do the Northern Lights manifest themselves in the Finnish sky?

   a) Like dancing shadows
   b) Like silent lightning bolts
   c) Like shooting stars
   d) Like rainbows at night

13) What is special about the first Finnish library?

   a) She was mobile.
   b) It was underground.
   c) It was built entirely of ice.
   d) It was reserved for kings.

14) How is the first snow in Finland described?

   a) Like a soft blanket
   b) Like tears from heaven
   c) Like a frosty mist
   d) Like a royal cloak

15) What is the source of the mysterious song of the Finnish land?

   a) Migratory birds
   b) The wind through the pines
   c) The Vibration of Tree Roots
   d) The Murmur of the Streams

16) What are the rituals of transition from childhood to adulthood associated with?

    a) Change of clothes
    b) Branding with a hot iron
    c) Traditional Ceremonies
    d) Offerings to the gods

17) How is Finnish natural ballet often described?

    a) Swirling Leaves
    b) Birds dancing in the sky
    c) The Flight of the Butterflies
    d) The movement of branches in the wind

18) What represents the inner strength of the Finns?

    a) Their ancestral traditions
    b) Diet
    c) The harsh climate
    d) Their sporting achievements

19) How is the first Finnish winter described?

    a) A never-ending white coat
    b) Freezing and cold weather
    c) A Period of Endless Festivities
    d) A moment of rebirth

20) Which tradition is considered a warm embrace by Finns?

a) Make a bonfire
b) Sing traditional songs
c) Take a sauna
d) Cooking traditional dishes

Answers

1) Where does the floor sing when touched?

Correct answer: d) Korouoma Marsh

2) What is the mythical animal that is supposed to inhabit Finnish lakes?

Correct answer: a) Dragon

3) What activity do Finns like to immerse themselves in despite freezing temperatures?

Correct answer: b) Snow bath

4) Who are considered the traditional custodians of Finnish houses?

Correct answer: c) Guardian spirits

5) What natural phenomenon is nicknamed "the dance of the fireflies in summer"?

Correct answer: d) Firefly Burst

6) What is the importance of elders in Finnish culture?

Correct answer: a) They are knowledge keepers.

7) What are traditional Finnish textiles made of?

Correct answer: c) Wool

8) What does snow look like when it sparkles in the Finnish sun?

Correct answer: c) To diamonds

9) Which river is known to have the peculiarity of flowing upside down?

Correct answer: d) Suttesaja River

10) Which legend is related to the protection of Finnish forests?

Correct answer: a) Guardians of the forest

11) What is the highly respected ancient art in Finland?

Correct answer: b) Weaving

12) How do the Northern Lights manifest themselves in the Finnish sky?

Correct answer: a) Like dancing shadows

13) What is special about the first Finnish library?

Correct answer: a) She was mobile.

14) How is the first snow in Finland described?

Correct answer: a) Like a soft blanket

15) What is the source of the mysterious song of the Finnish land?

Correct answer: c) The vibration of tree roots

16) What are the rituals of transition from childhood to adulthood associated with?

Correct answer: (c) Traditional ceremonies

17) How is Finnish natural ballet often described?

Correct answer: d) The movement of branches in the wind

18) What represents the inner strength of the Finns?

Correct answer: a) Their ancestral traditions

19) How is the first Finnish winter described?

Correct answer: b) Freezing and cold weather

20) Which tradition is considered a warm embrace by Finns?

Correct answer: c) Take a sauna

Printed in Great Britain
by Amazon